Flying Solo
A Practical Guide

*HOW TO REPRESENT
YOURSELF IN COURT
IN ENGLAND & WALES*

Chapter 3

ALEX WOODS

*For those brave souls
who represent themselves
in court.*

TABLE OF CONTENTS

Chapter 2 | Take-Off: Issuing & Defending Claims 105

Chapter 3 | Keeping the Plane in the Air: Case Management & The Proceedings

Chapter 4 | Fully Armed & Loaded: Disclosure, Court Orders & N244s

Chapter 5 | The Dogfight: Evidence & Trial

Chapter 6 | The Mindset of a Fighter Pilot: Tactics

Published by Redwood Legal Ltd
138-140 Southwark Street
London SE1 0SW

Warning – Disclaimer
The purpose of this book is to educate and entertain. The author and/or publisher do not guarantee that anyone following these techniques, suggestions, tips, ideas, or strategies will become successful. The author and/or publisher shall have neither liability nor responsibility to anyone with respect to any loss or damage caused, or alleged to be caused, directly or indirectly, by the information contained in this book.

ISBN: 978-1-71696-617-0 (print)

Editor: Kinga Stabryla
Junior Assistant Editor: Klaudia Jędrzejczyk
Cover design: Kinga Stabryla
Cover illustration: Nate Fakes
Book layout and design: Slaven Kovačević
Photographer: Kinga Stabryla

PREFACE

I have chosen to use the analogy of Fighter Pilots in this book. This seems, to me, the perfect metaphor for civil litigation as it helps a litigant in person to get into the right mindset. Whilst a pilot might have a very good aeroplane he might not be a very good pilot. He could, therefore, be defeated by an opponent in an inferior aeroplane with greater experience. In this analogy, of course, the case is the plane and the pilot is the individual running the claim. I have seen many good claims ruined because they were badly run or the individual found themselves up against a rich opponent who could afford clever lawyers. Combat in the skies is not something the Average Joe has any experience of, and the same is true of the complex procedural rules of civil litigation.

Only a fool would play the game without having learned the rules. Whilst you might get away with riding a skateboard, a bicycle or even driving a car without ever having any training, would you get into the cockpit of an aeroplane knowing what you are doing? Have you ever seen the inside of the cockpit of an aeroplane?! I doubt anyone could take off or land a plane properly without knowing what all those buttons on the consoles did.

Moreover, just as in the case of flying there are not only the laws of aerodynamics (the laws of the land), but there are also complex procedural rules with a whole system of air traffic control in place. So, it is that civil litigation has a complex set of rules, called the Civil Litigation Rules, brought in by Lord Woolf, by means of the Access to Justice Act 1999.

Now you could try and go it alone and I am certainly not saying that you have to know these rules in detail (key areas are dealt with in this book), but to get a real jump on your opponent it is worth dipping into them... or at the very least knowing that they are there, all freely available online. I say this because civil proceedings are a dogfight and it is those who play the game well who come away winners. I will cover an example or two of how you can turn these rules to your advantage later in the book.

It is important to understand that where civil litigation is concerned you are engaged in a solo activity in which the best man is likely to win. Sure, it is a big advantage to be in a spitfire rather than an old bi-plane from the first world war, but you are primarily engaged in an entrepreneurial and commercial endeavour – this is not about "justice" or other lofty ideals. It is about winning. Do not get engaged in civil litigation if you are just fighting for your rights or a just cause. That is the province of the rich, celebrities and media types. Even having a strong claim with real merit is not conclusive. It is simply just like having a spitfire. It will certainly make a difference, but it will not get you over the wire. It is a question of who is at the controls and what they do with the aeroplane.

So, do not do what most disgruntled claimants and defendants do. They suffer from the illusion that they can handle it all themselves and the court and the judge is somehow going to be entirely sympathetic and immediately see how badly they have been wronged and give them instant justice. Not true! Courts and judges are extremely busy and fortune favours the prepared. Facing a battle in court – just like life or an aerial dogfight – can be a complicated affair.

Unfortunately in civil litigation, you have to pay quite a lot of money to get a professional to take over the controls and fly the plane for you and in cases allocated to the small claims track you are unlikely to get your legal fees back, even if you win. This is probably why you are reading this book.

So this is your very own, "Paperback Wing Man."

Warning Note!

You need to make sure that any book or legal resource you use online is up to date. The law changes all the time! There were big changes to civil litigation in April 2013 and again in 2018 and since that time there have been many judgments that have updated and clarified those statutory laws. Here is an example of why this caveat could be important:

> **CASE STUDY: PERSONAL INJURY CLAIM**
>
> Let's say you have a personal injury claim. As things currently stand if it is under £1,000 for the physical damage itself then it will almost certainly be designated as a "small claim". This means you will not be liable to pay the legal costs of your opponent, even if you lose. Nor will they have to pay yours, if you instruct a lawyer. But under the recent Civil Liability Act 2018 this will almost certainly change and by the Spring of 2020 it could go up to £5,000, certainly for road traffic personal injury. So this danger of having to pay legal costs will only occur for a personal injury claim of above £5,000. A pretty significant change. Far more claimants will now run their own personal injury cases without legal help.

Alongside this book, we provide information on our website at www.courtwingman.com and YouTube channel to ensure you are kept up to date as well as provide you with supplementary materials.

Who is this book for?

This is a book for those individuals or small businesses, whether a claimant or a defendant, who have a civil dispute based in the jurisdiction of England & Wales and want to run the case themselves. Such people are called "litigants in person" to distinguish them from those claims where a lawyer has been instructed. There are increasing numbers of litigants in person in the courts these days and it is a growing problem: access to justice has been made more and more difficult by government cuts to the funding of the legal system, whether legal aid cuts or simple cuts to court staff and administration.

Flying the plane on your own may be the only real option if you have decided that it is un-economic to pay a lawyer to run it for you or if you distrust lawyers. But do you go into battle without any help at all?

This book will help you by giving guidance on how to run your claim. It may be a small, fast track or multi-track claim.[1] Cases which are over £25,000 are usually allocated to the multi-track, and those need a word of warning. They are likely to take a 2-day trial or more and involve more complex procedures. Frankly, I would advise you to take legal advice, although nothing is stopping you doing it yourself if you want to... just make sure you follow the rules provided in the Civil Procedure Rules. ("CPR".) I do touch on these claims in the book, and in many ways, they are no different to fast track claims (£10,000-£25,000), so it is relatively easy to cover them. But do please think carefully about obtaining at least a little judicious legal advice from a lawyer on the fast track and nearly mandatorily on the multi-track.

If your claim is a small claim and well under the £10,000 threshold (except for personal injury and housing disrepair[2]) then you need only read those sections that are relevant. The sections on legal costs will be less relevant for you because the normal rule on the small claims track is that the loser does not have to pay the winner's legal costs, which usually keeps lawyers out. But be careful about automatically assuming a low-value claim will always be allocated to the small claims track and that the rule about legal costs will always apply. Take note in particular of the first chapter in part 1 - "Small claims and allocation: a common misconception."

Who is this book not for?

This book is not for people with an employment dispute or a family dispute. Such cases are usually heard in special courts (the Employment Tribunal or Family Courts). Nor is this book for criminal matters.

Whilst it is of general assistance to those with personal injury claims (personal injury claims are civil claims heard in the county courts and

---

1   "Tracks" are what the courts put you on after you have issued a claim and they allocate to one of these three tracks in the vast majority of cases. Read on for an explanation of how these work.
2   Personal injury and housing disrepair claims are exceptions and have a lower threshold. Currently, this is £1,000 for personal injury claims in respect of physical injury, leaving aside any consequential losses of the injury and £1,000 for housing disrepair claims CPR 27.1(2).

so they share the same basic rules), you should be aware that the book does not specifically focus on this sector, which has a whole set of special rules and important changes happening. You are advised to look elsewhere for help with such claims if you need to go beyond the basics. You should also consider using a no win no fee lawyer, of which there are many and so you may well not need a guide book like this altogether.

There is also a whole range of other specialist claims where, frankly, you would be better off finding a lawyer to do it for you, certainly if you are forced to issue proceedings or are defending an issued claim. This could be a dispute of a high value such that it is allocated to the "multi-track" by the courts or it might simply be too complex for the layman. Examples might be intellectual property matters, libel, complex or large scale commercial disputes, contests wills and probate, and cohabitation property disputes (to name just a few).

At this point, I can almost hear you saying, "Surely the court system should be open to everyone?!" Of course, the court system should be open to everyone, however big or complex their case, and there have indeed been notable examples where litigants in person have managed their case. For example, as a young lawyer, I used to go and watch the famous "McLibel" case at the Royal Courts of Justice on The Strand. This was a case that two litigants in person defended themselves against the mighty McDonald's, and it lasted for months, if not years. It was a victory for them in one sense, as McDonald's failed to win on all counts, but they had to give up years of their lives to run it.

Despite this example and quite frankly, I have seen too many people get into hot water where there was high value or complexity involved, such that my general advice is to get a lawyer involved. There are always exceptions, of course, and I should perhaps add that I have on a few occasions had clients who had run their cases themselves initially, even issuing claims, and subsequently asked us to represent them when matters started to become complex. This saved them money because they only turned to the lawyers when necessary.

If your claim is complex, but not sufficiently high value to justify the use of lawyers then you may want to question whether it is wise to bring the claim in the first place. "Pick your battles", as they say.

What is this book's focus?

It is important that this not be an academic book but an entirely practical one and that you get a real sense of what it is like to be fighting the aerial battle in the civil courts. This book draws on real-life examples of cases that I have personally run in the county courts. Occasionally, I refer to these case studies in the book, highlighting them in their separate boxes so you can skip them if they are not relevant to your case. Over time I will be building a library of such cases on the website.

This is not intended to be a dry and technical exposition of the law on the procedure (there are plenty of other books that do this), but a real aid to fighting your case. As well as providing you with tools, a lot of what this book is about is giving you the courage to do it alone. I want you to know by the end of the book what it is like to have been in a dog fight.

It also does not focus on "substantive" law (Ie. the laws of the land). If you want a proper study of the elements of contract law, negligence, or misrepresentation then look elsewhere. There are plenty of solid academic tomes on the English law and you do not need me to add to the pile. This is what law students have to study but it is, in fact, surprisingly redundant when it comes to actual proceedings as disputes rarely centre on issues of law. In the vast majority of cases, the law is pretty clear and the battle is in fact about a whole range of other tactical, evidential, and procedural issues.

I do, however, deal with issues around the substantive law in the section on causes of action. This is because you may have the problem of complexity in your cause of action that prevents you from bringing a claim properly in the first place and so I devote a small section on it. It is important to have first bottomed out which "runway" to the courts it is you are using, as in certain cases without pleading your cause of action carefully you could run into trouble.[3] You do sometimes have to lay out the legal framework.

This book does not take a black and white viewpoint on whether or not to use lawyers to assist you in your case. For instance, you may wish

---

3   If there is serious legal complexity in your cause of action, this is another area where you will want to turn to a lawyer for help.

to use lawyers, on a limited, "advice-only" basis.[4] So this book is also a guide for individuals or businesses who want to have some involvement in their case but not use lawyers outright. The book will help you make the correct decision here.

Using lawyers is not an "either/or" situation, in my view. Many of my most successful cases are with clients to whom I have provided limited legal advice and assistance at key points of the litigation process, without actually going on the court record and formally representing them. Others have run the case themselves and then at a certain point in the litigation decided, perhaps for tactical reasons, to bring in the lawyers wholesale. This can be a smart tactical move, depending on the scale and complexity of the case. Since this book majors on tactics, it would be foolish to exclude one possible tactical move, which is simply to hand the case over to a law firm.

Indeed, if cash is tight, it may be that you need a lawyer who will represent you on a "no win no fee" basis. Even in small claims under £10,000 new "damages-based agreements" can sometimes be used. So, even if you have a small claim you might want to inform yourself about the different types of services lawyers can offer you - it is important tactically that you are aware of how lawyers can help. Using a lawyer judiciously could give you extra re-power in the battle to come.

And be in no doubt, a battle it is. You should be calm, cool and collected about it and present yourself professionally if you want to win.

---

4   Read below for more on this and how a lawyer can help you. The technical term for this type of retainer is "unbundled legal services" but I prefer the term "Lawyer Lite".

Chapter 3

KEEPING THE PLANE IN THE AIR: CASE MANAGEMENT & THE PROCEEDINGS

S o, we now move onto what I consider the third phase of civil litigation, which follows the completion of the statements of case. Both parties have clearly and concisely laid out their cases.

You are now well and truly "up in the air". You have made sure to launch your plane from the correct runway (cause of action) and into the right air corridor (Part 7, Part 8 or some other special procedure).[44]

Both parties will now have filed and served some or all of the below:

- ❖ Particulars of Claim
- ❖ Defence
- ❖ Reply to Defence
- ❖ Counterclaim
- ❖ Defence to counterclaim
- ❖ Reply to defence and counterclaim

---

44 There are some special courts and procedures that are outside the scope of this book. For instance contested will claims have to be brought in the special Chancery Courts and there is a very different procedure. Disputes around entrepreneurs and intellectual property have to be started in the Intellectual Property Courts, IPEC. Both are really quite different from the county court system.

It also goes without saying that you are now moving forward with real confidence in your case. You have laid the foundations of your case by following the pre-action protocol. You have tried alternative options for resolving the dispute prior to issue. You may well have made an offer. You are now moving forward without the bugbear of costs grinning over your shoulder. You need no longer be afraid of adverse costs implications that follow so many cases I deal with, where the case has not been properly laid out, pre-issue.

Part 18 Request

But, before I come on to the next phase I need to wrap up by touching on an additional weapon that many people are not aware of.

Now, the documents I listed above form the "pleadings" (old fashioned word) or "statements of case." (Same thing.) There is, however, one type of statement of case that is not included in the list above - a **"Part 18 Request".** It is rather a technical and unusual document and even lawyers rarely use it. I only use it in about 25% of my cases and usually only ever the once. You would probably not use it in a small claim, but definitely consider it for fast or multi-track.

Used judiciously, it can sometimes help unlock a certain issue so it is important that you know about its existence, at the very least. Think of it like a special missile that a fighter pilot would not normally use or need, but takes it with him just in case he envisages a tricky opponent.

Since we know that the Civil Procedure Rules are the basic touchstone for all things relating to civil proceedings, you will by now, of course, know that Part 18 refers to a specific section in them.

OBTAINING FURTHER INFORMATION 18.1

(1) The court may at any time order a party to – (a) clarify any matter which is in dispute in the proceedings; or (b) give additional information in relation to any such matter, whether or not the matter is contained or referred to in a statement of case.

Courts   Procedure rules   Offenders

Courts

Procedure rules

Civil

Rules & Practice Directions

PART 18 - FURTHER
INFORMATION

PRACTICE DIRECTION 18 –
FURTHER INFORMATION

Home » Courts » Procedure rules » Civil » Rules & Practice Directions »
PART 18 - FURTHER INFORMATION

PART 18 - FURTHER INFORMATION

Ministry
of Justice

Contents of this Part

Title	Number
Obtaining further information	Rule 18.1
Restriction on the use of further information	Rule 18.2

Obtaining further information

18.1

(1) The court may at any time order a party to –

(a) clarify any matter which is in dispute in the proceedings; or

(b) give additional information in relation to any such matter,

whether or not the matter is contained or referred to in a statement of case.

So, what is a Part 18? It is a way of forcing your opponent to go on record about a single issue, question, or point of information that they are avoiding answering.

Silence is a tactic often used by defendants. It can get you extremely frustrated as it forces you to spend more time and effort on getting to the bottom of the matter. You spend time getting or trying to get documents and information that you know they probably have but are deliberating hiding. Instead of making a special application to the court (via a N244, that will be covered later), which is expensive and time-consuming, it might be better to send the opponent a very carefully constructed question. It would be comparable to firing a laser-guided missile.

You see, the advantage of a Part 18 request is that it is considered part of the actual statements of case. So, it is a very important document that will sit with the other statements of case in the judge's file. It will not, therefore, be lost amongst all the other voluminous correspondence and evidence on file. You would in effect be saying that it is so important that it is a central plank of the case. Having said that, Part 18, much like any statement of case, should be a last resort if your opponent is refusing to engage. You should write to your opponent with a polite request and time-frame before making a formal request.

Now, let us take a construction dispute as an example. In the scenario, your opponent is a builder who built a wall in the wrong place, such that it actually trespasses onto a neighbour's property. He says he relied on an architect's drawing. You suspect that in fact there is a second drawing somewhere because you saw the first drawing and it was fine. Because of this, you suspect there were some shenanigans between the architect and the builder who, without your knowledge or consent, created a second drawing. This resulted in the wrongly positioned wall. Unfortunately, the architect is not part of the proceedings as the claim is against the builder for negligence. In the disclosure, the builder does not disclose the drawing. Similarly, the architect refuses to answer your correspondence about the issue. In such circumstances, you might actually want to write a Part 18 request. It would read,

"Was a second drawing of the works produced or was there only ever one drawing that the Defendant relied on in the construction works which are the subject of this dispute?" If the answer is yes, please supply the drawing and any relevant correspondence between the Defendant and the architect.[45]

Because a Part 18 request must be submitted in a certain format, it should be laid out in a separate document and signed. (see the Practice Direction CPR Part 18 for details.) Any reply must actually contain a sworn statement of truth because of the above reasons. Here is an example:

IN THE BRENTFORD COUNTY COURT   Claim No:

BETWEEN

MR JOHN SMITH

Claimant:

- and -

---

45 All my examples are based on real-life cases.

ACNE BUILDING SERVICES

<u>Defendant:</u>

CLAIMANT'S REQUEST
PURSUANT TO CPR PART 18

You are requested to provide the following further information or clarification under CPR Part 18 and the Part 18 Practice Direction:

1. Was a second drawing of the works produced or was there only ever one drawing that the Defendant relied on in the construction works which are the subject of this dispute?

If the answer is yes, please supply not only the drawing in question but any relevant correspondence between the Defendant and the architect relating to the creation of that separate drawing.

We look forward to your answer within 7 days and the supply of any documentation or correspondence within 21 days.

Signed

John Smith

Claimant

In addition, you will want to include a covering letter and file it all at court and formally serve it on your opponent. You could do that by email, or by post if they do not accept email service, or if you want to emphasise the importance of the document.

You need to give a time-frame for a response. I have given 7 days since the opponent hardly needs to think very long about it. But I have given a longer time period for the supply of documentation, which is only realistic, since he may have to persuade a busy and reluctant architect to supply correspondence. So 14 days might be another common time-frame.

Of course, a Defendant can make a Part 18 request as well.

Having now furnished you with the details of this additional weapon, that should not gather dust in your armoury, I will now come on to the third phase of litigation.

Summary Judgment & Default Judgment

This third phase is all about case management. The thing to remember here is you are going to have to liaise and even co-operate with your opponent. Think of it like two generals having a parley - white flags raised, battle temporarily suspended, all so that they can talk. Approach case management with your opponent with this frame of mind.

Before coming onto the directions questionnaire, which is the main tool used for this phase, I need to address two other matters that from time to time arise at this point. The first thing is a summary judgment and the second is a default judgment, (CPR Parts 24 and 12).

SUMMARY JUDGMENT

In practice, I rarely find that summary judgment is used.

Summary judgment is where a party is telling the court that, in their opinion, the defence or the claim (or a main plank or issue) does not stand and reach a basic threshold. In simple terms, it says the claim or the defence is so weak a judgment should be made early and the whole matter disposed of.

It rarely works. A judge is usually conservative and knows some evidence may appear at a later stage that will affect their decision – something he does not know about yet. So, he may be hesitant in giving a summary judgment. Also, the standard of proof is high, as you have to show that the defence or claim has no real prospect of succeeding. This is a lot higher than the usual balance of probabilities standard. You have to show that it is a "fanciful" claim or defence. Let us be honest, defences or claims are rarely "fanciful" - unless the person is a vexatious litigant. Therefore, bringing a claim for summary judgment may fail, expose you to unnecessary costs and prolong the proceedings.

DEFAULT JUDGMENT

Judgment in default is more common, especially in simple debt recovery claims. The classic example of use is where your opponent, usually the defendant, has failed to file on time. In simple money cases, where you are claiming for a specific amount of money, you can send a request to the court using a form called N255. You do not have to pay a fee. In more complex claims, you have to make a proper application using our friend, the N244, and paying the court fee (£255 at the time of writing).

You might think that getting a judgment in default is the end of it. Unfortunately, it is not. Judgments in default are easily set aside by a party making an application (yes, on an N244). A judge is likely to agree by accepting an excuse of some sort to not deny a party the chance to properly defend their case. If you think this is unfair, know that the court can also easily deal with the transgression. The judge will order costs against the party defaulting, rather than adopting any other, more draconian measures, like throwing out the case, which are rarely used. So, it is important to appreciate that the usual punishment for a breach of the rules are costs awarded against a party.

In terms of tactics, you might as well send an expensive barrister to a judgment in default hearing. He may just win the argument and even if he does not you will get your money back because of the defendant's failure in letting it get so far. It will hurt the other side because this may be the first time they actually have to put their hand in their pockets.

In civil litigation costs are a wonderful way of sobering up a stubborn-headed defendant. It jolts them into a settlement as often as not. To use the dogfight analogy, do not expect you are going to bring down your opponent in one skirmish. You are simply going to riddle his fuselage with bullets and give him a fright. This is enough.

If you get a paper judgment on default against a defendant, who could not be bothered to address your case, then note that this is not necessarily the end of the line for them. They can now make an "application for relief from sanction." This is found at CPR 3.9 and forms part of the court's general case management powers. You should definitely send an expensive barrister or a solicitor to such a hearing because you will almost certainly get your costs.

> **THE CREDIT CARD COMPANY CASE**
>
> It can be annoying generally that the courts let people miss deadlines and get away with it. I was involved in a case against a big credit card company and they just could not care less about the claim as it was low priority. They even insulted the judge by faxing through a letter an hour before the hearing saying it was too far to come. But even after we had judgment they still got it set aside by making an application for relief from sanction, even though it was a pretty flagrant breach.
>
> Guess what happened at that hearing? It was a different judge, who was not as annoyed as the first one and did not perhaps have the full picture as to how scurrilously the defendant had flouted the court. So, he set aside the judgment! It was all such a waste of time and money and it slowed up the case. The Defendant had effectively thrown a spanner in the works, so you could even argue it was a good tactical move! Although they had to pay our costs, they did not much care about the costs order against them because they were a large credit card company, and so for them it was a paltry amount.

Judges usually knock your costs down at such stand-alone hearings (called "interlocutory" hearings or interim hearings) so you do not actually get your full costs to boot. (See Chapter 5 on cost schedules.)

As I say, you need to accept that you may not win an individual battle on costs. But, if your opponent breaches court rules enough times it will put them on the back foot and they can eventually end up on the wrong side of a big costs order. It can be annoying how long it sometimes takes to get justice because of our underfunded court system. Still, if you make a few passes and each time score a cost hit your opponent is going to start to wobble. Costs will often be the thing that brings them to the negotiating table to agree to a reasonable settlement.

After all, very few cases actually get all the way to trial. In a dogfight, a party whose fuselage is riddled with bullets and guns are jammed would rather concede defeat and hurry back to base, rather than ditch into the sea!

Strike-Out Applications

Strike-out applications are far more common than summary judgments. They allow you to attack a legal or procedural error in order to get rid of a claim or a defence. Attacking procedural errors is more effective than attempting to just get the case kicked out for lack of merit. Although, it can also be used to draw the court's attention to how the claim or defence lacks merit. Lawyers love to use it against litigants in person because they are forever making procedural errors and do not appreciate how powerful costs can be as a weapon against them.[46] In the financial mis-selling cases I ran the banks would always reach for this weapon, even if there was no real merit in their application. It was done just to intimidate consumers.

Strike-out applications are made under CPR 3.4, yet another one of the court's case management powers. Technically a court can strike-out a case of its own volition but rarely does. You will need to do the heavy lifting. I have just pulled out the relevant criteria at the opening of this important section:

POWER TO STRIKE OUT A STATEMENT OF CASE 3.4

> (1) *In this rule and rule 3.5, reference to a statement of case includes reference to part of a statement of case.*
>
> (2) *The court may strike out (GL) a statement of case if it appears to the court –*
>   *(a) that the statement of case discloses no reasonable grounds for bringing or defending the claim;*

---

46 Litigants in person have the same burden when it comes to compliance with the CPR as I mentioned in the introduction, so do not think you can throw yourself on the mercy of the court.

(b) that the statement of case is an abuse of the court's process or is otherwise likely to obstruct the just disposal of the proceedings; or

(c) that there has been a failure to comply with a rule, practice direction or court order.

(3) When the court strikes out a statement of case it may make any consequential order it considers appropriate.

Strike-out applications are made the normal way, using the N244 in which you carefully, and concisely, state the issues or grounds for strike-out. You can copy and paste the above relevant section. You will then need to add a witness statement and exhibit in the statement evidence in which you say that you are right in your application.

The first reason for strike-out is the statement of case. If you are attacking it, attach it to the application or exhibit it in your statement. Make lots of lovely notes or markings on it to show why it is so ill-conceived and a mess. If you are saying it is a wrong cause of action state that in the N244 box (or attach an additional sheet) and then evidence the point in your statement. It also may be that the claim is limitations-barred and has been brought out of time. It could also be made where the wrong defendant is on the claim form, or there is a key missing defendant.

Another common reason for strike-out is the failure to particularise losses properly. It often occurs where claimants have tried to massage the figures into a preferred track, whilst it is clear they were trying to fit a round peg in a square hole. In more complex cases, I suggest you include a clear table when pleading your claim.

Hopefully you are starting to see why it is so important to get those pleadings right the first time and the importance of Part 2 of "Flying Solo".

Strike-out applications, the ones I see, are almost always made to attack a poorly-drafted claim or defence. It is like shooting fish in a barrel as far as an opponent's solicitors are concerned. Litigants in person so often make a dog's dinner of their claim or defence. Even when it is reasonably well-drafted, they tend to throw in the kitchen sink. What I mean by that is that they make them too long and load them all up with irrelevant issues. They often remind me of those old mechanical flying cars you find depicted by nutty inventors in Victorian drawings or something out of *The Wacky Racers* cartoon series. (Now you can start to see why I banged on about making your pleadings concise and focused in Chapter 2.)

Judges will not want to hurt a litigant in person too much by striking out the entire case. However, they will be more than happy to order costs against one and then require an amended statement of case to be filed within a tight time-frame. (See subsection (3), above.) I have seen a judge's order £1,000 or £2,000 costs against the losing party at the end of a 2-hour hearing and then give them 14 or 21 days to file a fresh, amended claim. In a situation like this, they had to grab for their lawyer. I have had to clean up many in such a situation. The shame is that it could all have been avoided had the claim been properly drafted the first time around.

Where your opponent is not represented by lawyers, you do not need to worry so much about strike-out, as they are likely to not be confident in making one. So, take what I say with a pinch of salt and make sure you have made a proper assessment of the risks. Having said that, if I were a sneaky litigant in person I would instruct a lawyer solely for the purpose of making such an application. Doing so would really frighten my opponent and bring them scurrying to the negotiating table.

If you are bringing your own strike-out application, make sure you do a statement of costs that you can bring to the hearing, so you can ask for costs at the end. (See Part 5, Costs Schedules.) Additionally, make sure you put your opponent on advance notice that you are going to make one by writing a letter or even sending them a draft of the application. Do not forget to give them a time period (7, 14, 21 days, etc.) within which you expect them to remedy the problem. For instance, if they have drafted the claim wrong, require them to apply to amend their claim (Form N244) and seek your consent to the amended statement of case. Also, ask for your costs of having to deal with the waste of time.

> ### A BUILDING DISPUTE
> We had a building dispute recently where a building company had damaged a wall of a property and the

owner, our client, had been forced to demolish it and build another, costing him £18,000. However, he drafted a voluminous and almost incomprehensible particulars of claim himself and he brought it in his own name, as the estate manager, rather than in the name of the actual owner, his brother. It even had inserts from emails, which are quite unnecessary and should have been left to the witness statement stage. We were only instructed late in the day, after witness statements had been exchanged, and barely 6 weeks before trial.

We negotiated a settlement. We only got the other side up to £6,500, and we strongly advised him to take it. This was chiefly because if he proceeded to trial with his wrong particulars, the other side (who had instructed reputable solicitors) might have made a strike-out application or the judge himself might unilaterally decided the claim needed amendment.

If that were to happen the judge would just rewind the clock and begin the whole process of disclosure and witness statements again. This would be doubling up work. The other side would then ask for their costs of this wasted work and the client would also have our bill to pay. So, we calculated the costs of this error at £5,000. It was simply not commercially intelligent to proceed further. It was best for him to take the £6,500 offer whilst it was on the table.

This is a classic and cautionary tale and one which illustrates how, at the end of the day, you have to take a commercial view.

Here is an illustration of how you might fill in the N244 for a strike-out application. It is just the key boxes (I furnish you with more details on how to fill out N244 forms in Chapter 4.)

N244

Application notice

For help in completing this form please read the notes for guidance form N244Notes.

Find out how HM Courts and Tribunals Service uses personal information you give them when you fill in a form: https://www.gov.uk/government/organisations/hm-courts-and-tribunals-service/about/personal-information-charter

Name of court		Claim no.	
Fee account no. (if applicable)		**Help with Fees – Ref. no.** (if applicable)	
		H W F – ☐☐☐ – ☐☐☐	
Warrant no. (if applicable)			
Claimant's name (including ref.)			
Defendant's name (including ref.)			
Date		1 Jan 2025	

1. What is your name or, if you are a legal representative, the name of your firm?

2. Are you a   ☑ Claimant   ☐ Defendant   ☐ Legal Representative

   ☐ Other *(please specify)*

   If you are a legal representative whom do you represent?

3. What order are you asking the court to make and why?

   An order that the Claimant's claim be struck out under CRP Part 3 (a) & (c).
   (a) that the statement of case discloses no reasonable grounds for bringing or defending the claim;
   (c) that there has been a failure to comply with a rule, practice direction or court order.

4. Have you attached a draft of the order you are applying for?   ☑ Yes   ☐ No

5. How do you want to have this application dealt with?   ☑ at a hearing   ☐ without a hearing

   ☐ at a telephone hearing

6. How long do you think the hearing will last?   2 Hours   ☐ Minutes

   Is this time estimate agreed by all parties?   ☐ Yes   ☑ No

7. Give details of any fixed trial date or period   Directions Questionnaires by 1 December

8. What level of Judge does your hearing need?   District Judge

9. Who should be served with this application?   The Claimant

9a. Please give the service address, (other than details of the claimant or defendant) of any party named in question 9.

N244 Application notice (08.18)   1   © Crown copyright 2018

10. What information will you be relying on, in support of your application?

☑ the attached witness statement

☑ the statement of case

☑ the evidence set out in the box below

If necessary, please continue on a separate sheet.
The Claimant claims that the final invoice of £12,500 has not been paid for building works (kitchen extension) that were carried out in October 2024.

(a) The reason that the invoice was not paid, as was explained in a letter we wrote to them on 1 November 2024, was because they left the site well before completion because they had problems with their business and had run out of money. As can be seen from the attached witness statement and exhibits (including photos of the unfinished kitchen and a report from an expert who inspected the works) the site was left in a terrible mess and they had not even put on the roof. As is detailed in our counterclaim we had to spend £4,500 to rectify problems with the works and £7,500 in completing the works.

(c) The claimant completely ignored the above letter and further emails and phonecalls and did not write to us at all pre-action, but simply issued proceedings without notice. They manfiestly failed to comply with the general pre-action protocol. This claim should be struck out and the claimant required to comply with the pre-action protocol and only then re-issue a claim.

Statement of Truth

(I believe) (The applicant believes) that the facts stated in this section (and any continuation sheets) are true.

Signed _____ Dated _____
                  Applicant('s legal representative)('s litigation friend)

Full name _____

Name of applicant's legal representative's firm   _____

Position or office held _____
(if signing on behalf of firm or company)

11. Signature and address details

Signed _____ Dated _____
                  Applicant('s legal representative's)('s litigation friend)

Position or office held _____
(if signing on behalf of firm or company)

Applicant's address to which documents about this application should be sent

	If applicable	
	Phone no.	
	Fax no.	
	DX no.	
Postcode ☐☐☐☐ ☐☐☐	Ref no.	
E-mail address	@googlemail.com	

2

Directions Questionnaire

When a bunch of planes took off in the Second World War they often made for a rendezvous and grouped together, before flying in a formation to meet the enemy.

Once you have filed and served all the different statements of case listed in Part 2, you have completed the "pleadings" phase. You are now not only in the air but at a flying altitude and about to reach a rendezvous point. This phase is one in which you, working together with your opponent and the court, organise and prepare the route ahead to trial. Unlike in the analogy of the fighter pilots, you are now liaising with your enemy! Yes, you do need to work with them and co-operate at the directions questionnaire stage.

This is an important thing to be aware of. In litigation, like any good lawyer, you should be wearing two hats. You should be super professional, and although they are the enemy it is especially important at this point that you have a little bit of a truce. Liaise and negotiate with one another, as you are required to do under the Civil Procedure Rules.

You need to agree to the next steps. Draw out the lines of the battle like two referees. For this, you should be entirely neutral at points in the discussion. This is not easy for a lot of people, but you do need to try and take a dispassionate view of your case at such times.

The court will send out a directions questionnaire to the parties to fill in and return to court. This is an important document, the map of the route ahead, and so you should take it seriously. The court may also propose a track that the case should be allocated to. In small claims, there is a special directions questionnaire for the management of small claims (N180). If you receive it then the court thinks it should be allocated to this track. If you do not want this you should be very clear about this in the questionnaire. You should also inform your opponent and attempt to get them to agree to the same track that you want. Once you agree, you should both use the N281 form for the fast track and the multi-track, not the small claims track one. Just because the court has sent out an N180, it does not mean you are duty-bound to use it. The court will be more than happy for the parties to agree on something different. If you do not agree, it will be happy to hear an application, via a short telephone hearing or otherwise, to decide on the issue you disagree on. But the starting point is putting your case strongly on the actual questionnaire.

DIRECTIONS QUESTIONNAIRE 26.3

(1) If a defendant files a defence –
 (a) a court officer will –
  (i)   provisionally decide the track which appears to be most suitable for the claim; and
  (ii) serve on each party a notice of proposed allocation; and
 (b) the notice of proposed allocation will –
  (i)   specify any matter to be complied with by the date specified in the notice;
  (ii) require the parties to file a completed directions questionnaire and serve copies on all other parties;
  (iii) state the address of the court or the court office to which the directions questionnaire must be returned;
  (iv) inform the parties how to obtain the directions questionnaire; and
  (v)   if a case appears suitable for allocation to the fast track or multi-track, require the parties to file proposed directions by the date specified in the notice.

Track Allocation

One of the most important decisions to be made and agreed upon at this stage is allocation. So, here is a refresher and additional information to supplement what I said in the introduction.

Remember that a claim is not a small claim until it is allocated as such. Many claims fall on the cusp of £10,000 and so you have a tactical decision to make here. You can also bet a smart opponent will be thinking about things tactically. You need to consider that the case may not be appropriate for small claims because of a special factor, as I explained in an earlier part of the book series.

You also need to think about the dangers of a counterclaim, which could take the value of the claim (for allocation purposes) above the small claims limit. It is a factor the court will take into consideration. If you disagree with the court at this stage you can apply to have your claim re-allocated.

As I have already explained there are tactical advantages to either party. You will have to make a very important decision if your claim value is knocking around the £10,000 mark and there is clearly ambiguity over whether it is actually a small claim or not.

TICKET INSPECTOR VS MBNA CREDIT CARDS

I sued MBNA Credit Cards on behalf of a Ticket Inspector with Transport for London, for a sum around the £10,000 mark. The cause of action was technical, so he really could not fight this finance case without legal representation. MBNA wanted to get it onto the small claims track, because that would make fighting for the case virtually financially unviable for my client. He would still need a lawyer to win and because of the rules of the small claims track he would not get his legal costs paid by MBNA even if he did win. These legal costs were likely to be double the claim value and the banks were wise to this during the financial crisis, when they were faced with a lot of disgruntled consumer claims. So, they made a point of fighting even weak cases all the way to trial and only ever settling at the courtroom doors. They did this precisely for this tactical reason.

The court allocated it to the small claims track – it saw £10,000 and considered it was a small claim. (Or rather a court clerk did.) We decided to appeal the allocation decision and applied for a specific hearing just on allocation. We won it. It was a complex claim and, in fact, it ended up being split into two trials: one of the merits of the case, whether MBNA had broken the law and mis-sold a financial product, and the second on the amount of the claim

> – quantum. Each hearing was about half a day long on two separate days – given a total trial length of one day, which is the standard for a fast track case. He won his claim and the cost of around £20,000 was also paid by MBNA to us.

So, you may want it allocated to the small claims track for the reverse reason. The above case was a no win no fee one so the client was not having to cash flow the litigation. But, what if the claim is a simple one of value around £10,000 against a builder who has lawyers? He wants it allocated to the fast track so that you have the serious threat of paying £20,000 if you lose your case. It is a simple tactic of intimidation.

Even if you think you have a good case, you may be nervous about this danger. Can you afford to go all the way to a trial, where you might lose or fail to accept an offer that later turns out to be a good one (see Part 36 offers, Part 6 of the series)? And on top of this, you may have the £20,000 bill for your own lawyers as well, if you decide that you cannot fight the case without them once it is on the fast track.

So, in such cases you want the court to allocate it to the small claims track. How do you maximise your chances? The directions questionnaire asks you many other general questions about how to manage the case. One key area is the trial length. The shorter the trial, the bigger the likelihood of it landing on the small claims track.

The questionnaire will also ask you how many witnesses you want to call. If you want to call more than just yourself, for example, one expert or one other witness, this may affect the allocation decision. In a small claim there should rarely be more than your opponent and yourself giving evidence, and perhaps a single, joint expert or one other witness each. But if it looks as if there will be 4 witnesses, who are going to have to turn up at court (some witness statements can be agreed and read), you will be in danger of going into a whole day trial. If so, the court may then allocate it to the fast track. Usually, one witness in addition to yourself and a joint expert is the maximum for a small claim. A half-day trial is not going to be able to cope with a bunch of witnesses – they are time-consuming. So, focus on only essential witnesses, like yourself, if you want a small claim allocation.

The other issue is complexity. In some of the financial mis-selling cases I handled there were a lot of financial documents and often a cause of action that was alien to most judges. You needed a barrister to explain it all and lay out the law. Such causes of action (such as the Unfair Relationships Test Consumer Credit Act 2006) were legally complex and an hour or so was needed to lay out the law the bank had allegedly broken. Thus, you might want to refer to the complexity in the directions questionnaire to help the court make a decision.

Note that you are inviting the judge to make directions about the future conduct of the proceedings. You may, therefore, want to include information about the need for certain very important disclosure, experts, a response to a Part 18 request, and so on. You may also want to ask the court for a hearing to discuss and debate on these matters, rather than having the court send out Pro-forma directions on paper.

As well as a decision on trial length and witnesses you need to think about whether you want a stay (pause) to attempt to settle or for some other reason. If you have a small claims track case you will be able to tick a box for using the court mediation service. You should usually tick this. Then, a member of the court staff will list a phone call in which they will talk to you both and attempt to get you to meet in the middle. It is not a proper mediation, more a case of banging heads together.

Do not feel obliged to settle – the important thing at this point is that you have agreed to mediate and so headed off the danger of a judge criticising you for not even trying.

If it is a fast-track or multi-track claim you will want to tick the box for a month's stay to allow for proper mediation with an independent mediator. This can be expensive, especially if lawyers are involved and mediation takes a whole day. You will then face costs for two lawyers, one mediator, and three hired rooms (aim to split the costs in half). This could easily turn into a £4,000 or £5,000 exercise. The mediator might cost £1,200, room £500, and the lawyers £1,000 each.

Even though it is expensive, the courts encourage out of court settlements and aim to decrease the number of cases landing at court. Therefore, it is usually important to try. Why? Because should you refuse and your opponent asks for it, a judge could take a dim view when deciding on that big old bugbear of civil litigation – costs. Mediation takes place in total confidence, where you can freely make offers. The judge will not know what has gone on, until after the main trial – in other words, most likely never.

You may have chosen mediation early on, for example in a complicated, high-value building dispute. But, if you have not done mediation pre-issue do not worry. You can try it at this phase of the proceedings, by asking for a stay.

You can see from all the above that you will have to make a lot of case management decisions. This is not the time to attack your opponent's case or beef up yours. Be professional, neutral, and liaise with your opponent, and do not be afraid to pick up the phone. Use the above section to help you think about what is important for your case in terms of managing the future proceedings, for instance:

❖ I want it allocated to a certain track;
❖ I want an expert and want permission;
❖ I want some key disclosure;
❖ I want a hearing to deal with allocation and the directions questionnaire because it is complex;
❖ I want a hearing because myself and my opponent have a fundamental disagreement on how the case should be managed;
❖ Some other issue.

This last item could cover a range of things that are unique to your case. One example could be where your opponent's statement of case is deficient but you do not want to go to the lengths of making an application to strike it out. You could raise this in the directions questionnaire and invite the judge to order your opponent to apply to amend. Remember that the judge has powers to manage a case and this can include striking out a case of his own volition.

Think about the wording of the court order you want the court to produce that will assist you. (I cover court orders further down.) Indeed, sometimes a draft court order is attached to the directions questionnaire.

Having formed a view of what directions you want to make, remember that you must then liaise with your opponent to attempt to get their consent. Do not get too personal. Instead, write emails or letters along the following lines:

"Dear Sirs

We were contacted by the court who has sent us a notice of proposed allocation to the small claims track. We do not believe that this is the right track. There is a counterclaim from you and it looks as if an expert will also be needed. In terms of trial length, we believe the trial will take one day, especially since it is likely that there will be two additional witnesses, on top of the expert.

Please confirm your agreement to invite the court to allocate the matter to the fast track and that you will be filling out the fast track questionnaire. You can easily find it online. We attach a draft copy of the proposed order for convenience.

Please also note that, as raised in earlier correspondence, we believe it is essential that you answer our Part 18 question (dated X) and provide the document requested.

As we believe that the fast track is the right track, we will be filling in form N181 and not the N180, the form the court initially sent out."

If they do not get back to you, mention this fact in your directions questionnaire. It helps to make you look professional and professionalism is key in civil litigation - judges love it! You may even want to flourish the letter at the next hearing to show how your opponent has not been working with you to manage the claim expeditiously. In a way, all these documents are comparable to you laying a mine – it will not hurt your opponent now and they will often ignore it but it can be detonated later.

So, do not get too frustrated if nothing happens and the court is not proactive at this early stage. Bide your time. If that key document only arrives at trial you can produce the letter and the part 18 requests and hand it to the judge. He will be very unimpressed with the other side. Also, if this conduct meant you have not been able to prepare your case he may vacate the hearing and order costs against the opponent.

Key points:

❖ If you do not have the correct directions questionnaire, it is easy to find using your internet browser;

❖ You need the N180 for a small track claim or an N181 for a fast or multi-track claim;

❖ Liaise with the opponent and agree on things before asking for court's help;

❖ Check that your opponent is using the correct questionnaire if you have both agreed to the same track, and

❖ Be professional and use formal means of communication for convenience.

Budgets & Precedent H

You may have a higher value claim and think that your case is on the multi-track. This will be the *normal* track for claims above £25,000 and the trial length is typically 2 days. Therefore, you may be worried that you have to comply with the CPR and produce a "Precedent H" as the N181 form for fast and multi-track claims requires. But do not worry about this cumbersome, complicated document, even if your claim is on the multi-track. Take a look at this section on the N181 questionnaire:

H Costs	Notes

Do not complete this section if:
   1) you do not have a legal representative acting for you
   2) the case is subject to fixed costs

If your claim is likely to be allocated to the Multi-Track form Precedent H must be filed at in accordance with CPR 3.13.

I confirm Precedent H is attached. ☐

So, you do not need to do this if you are unrepresented (CPR 3.13). But you still should require your opponent to include theirs, if they are. You can then go through it and challenge their costs as being too high at the costs and case management hearing. Unlike in lower value claims, you will often have a specific hearing to deal with the management of costs, and Precedent Hs are key. Multi-track claims are complicated by the way, in all sorts of ways, and these weirdly titled cost schedules, "Precedent Hs", are a good example.

Frankly, any multi-track client really does need the services of a lawyer, or at least some kind of legal guidance. If you are running your own multi-track claim you will need to swot up on the rules and read CPR Part 29 and others. At the costs management hearing the costs schedules will be ruled on by the judge, often as part of a general management hearing for the case itself.

I am going to go into Precedent Hs now to give you an overview. Even though you are not required to complete one, you should be aware of its dangers. You can then use it as a helpful reference for how the courts are operating these days, so you do not get taken by surprise. You may also even want to do your own mini-budget if you have your own costs, legal and otherwise. For instance, you may have used a lawyer for the pre-action stage, then run out of money and de-instructed them to run the case yourself. You can claim these costs back and you should bring them to the attention of the court.

WHY DO WE HAVE PRECEDENT HS?

There are specific costs rules governing multi-track cases, found in Part 3 of the CPR. (Note that they are for Part 7 claims, so a Part 8 claim may not need to comply.) A few years ago the powers decided that litigation should be reformed and structured in the same way you might run any building project. What this means is that you have to cost each stage before the work begins - be accountable and transparent.

So, you have to commit to telling the court and your opponent, by means of this schedule, what legal fees are going to be spent on each stage (statements of case, disclosure, witness statements, trial, etc.). This is done in an attempt to control costs and reduce the danger of a blank cheque, where lawyers keep on running up a bill with no accountability. Once you have won the case you will not get more than you put into your budget, unless there are exceptional circumstances.

I can tell you that your opponent will attempt to load up the Precedent H with as many costs as they can muster. They will try and get away with as much as they can, just like a dodgy construction company with a client who is a little green around the ears. (Lawyers are not perfect.) So you should, at least, think about challenging these costs – it might be worth getting a lawyer to give you advice on this specific aspect alone. There is, in fact, a document called a "Budget Discussion Report". It is a template provided by the courts which narrows the issues of dispute around the contents of a Precedent H. I would not suggest you fill this in, but do write a list of unreasonably high costs your opponent listed so that you can bring it to the judge's attention.

My personal view is that trying to fill in complex forms like this gets you into a muddle. It is far better to try and produce one simple A4 page which lays out your costs and email it as a PDF or print it out. If you take my advice, you might also then want to write down the key areas of your opponent's costs you object to on a separate page. A judge will try and be helpful at a Costs or Case Management Hearing but remember they are very busy. Unless you bring specific points to their attention they may overlook them. At that hearing, they will make an order approving a certain level of costs. (Again, a bit like a quantity surveyor in a building dispute.) Solicitors are very protective about their costs, of course, and do not like being knocked down so keeping them on a tight budget will make them disgruntled. If they see that you are organised they may become concerned about the case generally. Litigants in person are often seen as a costly nuisance by lawyers and so do not be afraid! They also fear you!

If you are on the fast-track you will find a Precedent H at the Practice Direction 3E. It is actually attached as an annex.

You will also find some Guidance Notes produced by Justice.gov. uk if you search for them on your Internet browser.

Draft Directions

In fast track and multi-track cases, the parties are expected to agree on directions. You should draft an order and include a hard copy with the directions questionnaire. The judge will be able to amend it in court.

Do not worry if your claim is going to be allocated to the small claims track. If it is, you will have been sent the small claims questionnaire, where there is no need to include additional directions drafted up into a separate document.

Typically lawyers would create their special template-form of directions with legalese in it, but as a litigant in person, it is enough to draw up a list of the things you want. Hopefully you can agree on directions together. If not, send your own form and let the court decide. For fast track claims the court is likely to lay down a timetable on its own initiative. If you are up against a law firm, try and get them to produce draft directions which you can then read, amend and send back - even if you are the claimant. This is the time to be professional and liaise with your opponent. So, say to the other side "You are lawyers, you know how to draft these things, get one done and let me check it". You want to make sure that the draft order is asking for everything you need.

This is an example of draft directions, taken from an actual case:

IN THE BRENTFORD COUNTY COURT   Claim No:

B E T W E E N:

MR JOHN SMITH

Claimant

-and-

ACNE BUILDING SERVICES

Defendant

CLAIMANT'S PROPOSED DIRECTIONS

BEFORE District judge / Deputy District judge

UPON the Parties having agreed to the terms of this order

BY CONSENT;

IT IS ORDERED that:-

1. The Claim is allocated to the fast track;

2. The matter be stayed for a period of 3 months in order that the parties can explore a resolution to the dispute by means of mediation;

3. Should mediation be unsuccessful standard fast track directions shall apply:

4. Each party shall give the other standard disclosure of documents by serving copies together with a disclosure statement no later than 1 November 2019;

5. Each party shall serve on each other and file at court the witness statements of all witnesses of fact upon which they intend to rely. There be simultaneous exchange of such statements no later than 15 November 2019;

Expert

6. It appears to the court that expert evidence is necessary in the field of legal finance, that evidence be given by a single expert instructed jointly by the parties, the parties shall inform the court no later than 1 December 2019 whether such an expert has been instructed. If the parties cannot agree about who the expert should be by that date they shall apply forthwith to the court for directions;

7. A joint letter of instruction shall be sent to the expert by 15 December 2019;

8. The joint expert will report to the parties by 1 January 2020;

9. The parties may put written questions to the joint expert by 15 January 2020;

10. The joint expert will respond to questions by 1 February 2020;

Trial

11. Each party shall file a completed pre-trial checklist by 15 February 2020;

12. The matter is to be listed for trial with a 1 day time-frame on the first available date after 15 February 2020;

13. Standard directions as to trial bundles, skeleton arguments, case summary etc. shall apply;

14. Costs in the case.

Dated:

Signed ....   Signed ....

      Claimant   Defendant

On the other hand, below is an example of an order produced by the court for a standard fast-track case, after it has reviewed the directions questionnaire or held the case management hearing. You can use it as a checklist for the sort of things you need to think about.

If, following strike out of the claim the claimant or defendant wishes to start fresh proceedings a new claim must be filed together with the appropriate fee or application for help with fees.

Information and leaflets explaining more about how to pay a court fee or how to apply for a help with fees are available from the court office **or online at:** https://www.gov.uk/court-fees-what-they-are

The trial fee is **non refundable**. If parties settle before the trial fee is due, the trial fee will not be payable. If a consent order settling the matter is requested after the trial fee has been paid, the consent order fee will still be payable.

Please note, unless you apply for help with fees, there will be no further correspondence from the court office regarding payment of the fee or warnings as to the consequences of non payment.

1. The Claim is allocated to the Fast Track

2. Standard disclosure of Documents will be dealt with as follows:

   a. By 4pm 22 July 2019 both parties must give each other standard disclosure of documents by list.

   b. Written notice will be made by 4pm on 29 July 2019 to request inspection.

   c. Any such request, unless objected to, must be complied with within 14 days of the request.

3. The parties have permission to rely on the jointly instructed written evidence of an Expert survey or in respect of the

quality and costs of the work that are the subject of this claim and counterclaim.

a. The experts report will be confined to the following issues:

Quality of work undertaken relevant to the claim and counterclaim.

Cost of work undertaken relevant to the claim and counterclaim.

By 10 July 2019 the parties must agree on the identity of the experts.

The parties shall send a joint letter of instruction to the expert by expert by 4pm on 12 August 2019.

By 4pm on 23 September 2019 the expert will report to the instructing parties.

By 4pm on 07 October 2019 the parties may put written questions to the expert.

By 4pm on 28 October 2019 the expert will reply to the questions.

A copy of this order must be served on the expert by the Claimant with the expert instructions.

A party seeking to call the expert to give oral evidence at trial must apply for permission to do so before pre-trial checklist are filed.

Unless the parties agree in writing or the Court orders otherwise, the fees and expenses of the expert will be paid by the parties giving instructions for the report equally.

4. Witness statements will be dealt with by simultaneous exchange.

By 4pm on 11 November 2019 both parties must serve on each other copies of the signed statements of themselves including witness statements.

5. Pre trial checklists must be filed by each party by 4pm on 27 November 2019.

6. The matter shall be listed for a trial on 06 January 2020, with a time estimate of 1 day.

It is quite detailed, is it not?

It is from a case of a litigant in person who had a claim of around £15,000 and was running it himself at this point. He later decided to instruct us to represent him.

Experts

Experts are brought into court to give the judge an opinion or explain a process within their area of expertise. They are most commonly used in building disputes, where the judge needs to know whether something is defective or not. They are pretty important and, using an example, I will demonstrate why below.

WHY ARE EXPERTS IMPORTANT?

This is best explained using an example.

> **BUILDER VS CLIENT**
> At the time of writing, we have a building case at the law firm. It is between our client and a builder who made errors. The builder does not agree errors were made. Since the client is sure errors were made, we asked the

court to allow an expert (more on how to get one later). The expert has now evaluated the work done and produced a report in which he said the other side has made errors.

Having this on paper gives us a big advantage. All things considered, he now feels the possibility of the judge being on our side and the risk of losing. It now means we have the builder on the back-foot. We can make an aggressive offer and warn him that if he continues to fight he will only be racking up a bigger legal bill than the claim value itself. He may have ignored our client, but he really cannot fight an independent expert who would not twist the truth and risk ruining his reputation.[47]

Of course, experts do not only apply to building disputes. They take part in any claim involving a situation where reasonable industry standards and procedures are set. For example, one may explain a set of procedures expected of a legal accountant in a dispute between a solicitor and an accountant.

HOW DO YOU GO ABOUT GETTING ONE?

You should consider the need for an expert before you fill out your directions questionnaire, as this is where you ask the court for permission. Their involvement is not automatic.

Like with any procedural matter, where you need to act professionally, it is wise to inform the opponent that you want an expert beforehand. You want them to also request an expert and cover half the fees so there is no possibility of someone claiming that the expert is biased.

---

47 You feel for the builder! I mean, to have some expert trawl over all your work with a microscope and check it against all the regulations and health and safety rules must be hard. I bet if all the building works that have ever been done came to court about 50% of them would be found to be negligently done, even though things still work and the building still stands up.

Once you have the green light, you should agree on directions with the opponent. If you have not done so, you should get the court to order directions in relation to it, if they have not already done so.

Then it is time to find a suitable expert. Those who already testify at court are most suited for this. Try to find 3 experts and request their CVs and costs. After you have collated their details, send them to the opponent and allow them to choose one. In small and most fast-track claims, you invariably will have only one expert on whom you will both agree. It is only in the bigger cases, on the multi-track, that you may have two experts. Doing it this way makes the process easier.

Once you agree, they are then jointly instructed, with each of you paying half their fees. If this is not possible, you will have to bear the costs. Yet, note that you can get your costs back on the small claims track if you win. Costs are currently capped at £750.

Experts usually occur before witness statements are exchanged but after disclosure.

Small Claims

Although a claim allocated to the small claims track has to follow the same law and procedure as any claim, there are distinctive features that merit emphasis.

Here are the basics you need to be aware of:

1) Personal Injury and Housing Disrepair Claims have lower thresholds than the £10,000. Since this area of law is very fluid at the moment I am not going to give you actual thresholds. Please search for CPR 26.6 using your internet browser to check where you stand. You need to also remember that this is not the only criterion for a case to be on the track (see "Track Allocation" section).

2) A small claim is not a small claim until it is allocated as such. So, you are still vulnerable to costs orders early on, such as when an application to strike out your claim is brought.

3) A party cannot get their legal costs paid by their opponent if they win. This means the involvement of lawyers is rare, but they are not banned altogether. I have illustrated this in the track allocation section above, where I gave an example of banks fighting small claims for policy reasons only. They know that civil litigation is a dogfight and in complicated claims like financial mis-selling they can run rings around an opponent, even when their opponent is flying a spitfire.

There is an exception to this rule if a party has behaved unreasonably. This rule would apply if you think that your opponent is fighting a weak case just to be vexatious or they have badly conducted proceedings.

4) You can claim other, non-lawyer costs, such as:

❖ Expert fees (current limit £750);
❖ Travelling expenses and other expenses – for example, a hotel if you have had to travel far;
❖ Time taken out of work up to a limit of £95 per day;
❖ Expenses and costs of witnesses;
❖ Court fees.

5) There is no disclosure phase and no rule that you have to disclose evidence that hurts your case. You just exchange witness statements and evidence on an appointed day that the court orders, usually 14 days before the trial;

6) Trial length. The time for small claim trials is half a day, so 10 pm-1 pm, for example. It will be the same judge and same court as for other tracks, but it may be in his chambers and more informal;

7) Total costs exposure. I would estimate that for a case nearing the high end of this range (costs are on a sliding scale for most types of claims for a purely monetary remedy) you are looking at an exposure of £1,000 maximum costs if you lose. These are mostly court fees and if it is a tiny claim this goes down to as low as £100. (Google "EX50" for details of what the current, exact costs are.) Costs can also be incurred if have to pay for an expert (maximum of £750) and loss of earnings for your opponent and his witnesses (£95 a day);

8) Make sure you have been genuinely wronged and you are not getting counter-claimed. If the case is low value and may be counterclaimed,

consider putting it down to experience this time. It could end up being more time- consuming and expensive than you imagined;

9) "Should I take legal advice?", you may be asking. Well, the system is designed to exclude lawyers but there are good eggs who will give you advice and not charge you an arm and a leg.[48] In higher value low claims you may even be able to persuade a law firm to represent you on a "Damages-Based-Agreement", where they are not charging you but simply taking a share of your winnings. (See Chapter 6.) It might be worth it if you trust them and use them judiciously in proportion to the size of the claim.

I ran a small claim before I was a lawyer and found it worked well. The value was £2,000. I went to his home town where the case was transferred (as is common if your opponent is not a company). I paid a small amount for fees. He did not show up. I got judgment and he paid up after a few weeks! Remember, that the most important thing is paperwork and preparation. So before you issue, you should have basically laid out exactly what the complaint is and what you want them to do to correct it and give them time to respond.

I have done a video on small claims on YouTube, which covers all the above basics. Just go on YouTube and find our channel "Redwood Legal".

---

48 Yes, ours!

Appendix

NO WIN NO FEE

I discussed retainers in the book and this type of particular retainer is important for litigants in person to be aware of. I have taken over cases that my clients have been running on their own and done it on a discounted or fully „no win no fee" basis. If you can get a lawyer to look at the possibility of a contingency arrangement, or "no win no fee", then this is very good – it may well be preferable than a traditional taxi meter rate, for obvious reasons. You will probably have to pay them to look at the case first so they form a view it is a strong one.

Above all „no win no fee" changes the relationship between you and the lawyer. It turns them into your business partner, which means they are highly incentivised to get a good result for you, rather than just letting the meter run. This is, therefore, a very good way of weeding out the conscientious lawyers from the gravy-train ones. You will have to pay them to look into your case initially, but once they feel it is strong they should at least be prepared for contingency or conditional fee arrangements.

Not all cases are suitable for contingency fee deals, but hopefully by the end of this section you will have got a handle on whether your case is. The basic reason for this is that it works only where there is a clear, identifiable pot of gold at the end of the case that a lawyer can leverage. This ensures that once the case is won there will be a guaranteed payment. For example, a property or an estate in a will dispute, or a big corporation who will not have difficulty finding the money.

NEGLIGENCE

Let's take an example that is based on a case I am currently running at time of writing. A client had asked us for preliminary advice on a £15,000 claim for which he paid £450 + VAT. At a later date he came back to us and wondered whether we would handle the entire case for him. He was finding the case against a very determined builder challenging. He was also exhausted from the fight and feeling he was just too close to his own case.

A lot of complexities had arisen around the negligence and there was a need to amend the claim. It transpired that a wall had been moved across a neighbour's property without planning consent. In other words, in light of the information, we needed to "beef up" the claim by an application to amend, using our old favourite, the N244.

We were able to offer him a 'no win no fee' deal for this, which we did at the disclosure phase. Because we had done that initial piece of advice and felt he had a strong case, we were happy to do this. When engaged we could also, of course, carefully calibrate a Part 36 offer, to boot – like launching a laser guided missile.

Any self-respecting law firm should do a review before it enters into a 'no win no fee' deal. It can be risky for a law firm not least because it can take so long until they see any money and need to cash flow a case. A law firm has to be convinced that it is a strong case. (The exception to this is the personal injury sector where large 'factory' firms can just "play the odds" and take on all sorts of cases.)

Tactically the use of 'no win no fee' retainers can be powerful and that is why I say any self-respecting law firm should be prepared to enter into them. It signals to your opponent that:

❖ A law firm specialising in litigation is now chasing them down;

❖ The law firm is hungry and are highly motivated to win as much as possible and as quickly as possible because they will not get paid until they do, and

❖ There may be a large legal bill that could double the costs of the whole proceedings if he were to lose.

So, here you can see how instructing a law firm can be a purely tactical decision. It is a little like radio-ing in an extra Spitfire against a particularly tricky Messerschmitt. He might suddenly turn tail and flee. And in this case the extra Spitfire has not cost you any extra money because he has agreed only to be paid if he wins – from a share of the spoils.

The Background

Over the past few decades the principle of proportionality of costs has led to a move in the direction of not just fixed fee regimes and budgets for running cases, but also towards "contingency" or "conditional" fee agreements. In 2013, the government expanded the 'no win no fee' regime and added a more American-like element which was the creation of what are called, "Damages-Based-Agreements". I am personally an advocate of them, if the case is right. What I like about them is that they turn the law firm into a business partner, rather than a taxi who just lets the meter run indefinitely. (On a trip where you do not know the destination or how long it will take!)

In contingency fee cases the lawyer does not get paid, or charges only a discounted rate, unless he gets you a result. Whether he gets paid or not is "contingent" on the result - in other words it depends on the outcome. Many law firms do not like them for this very reason. The additional problem is that you have to wait a long time for your money even if your case is successful. If you have ever run a business you will understand the adage that "cash is king". The value of cash now is worth ten times more than some possible cash that may come to you at some indefinite time in the future. And so lawyers do not like this arrangement. Fair enough. Cases can take years to reach court and even after victory there is the problem of recovery.

I should say, of course, that there are law firms that specialise in "no win no fee" exclusively. But this is usually limited to the personal injury sector.

I will give you a quick lesson in all of this and the short and dirty of the "skinny" on these contingency arrangements, which more properly deserve a book in their own right.

The Skinny on "No Win No Fee": The Treasure Island Analogy

I will use an analogy to try and explain how these complex types of retainers work. It applies in the ease of "no win no fee" or a "conditional fee agreement", something that we have had for the last 30 years.

Let's say you have a treasure map (a good case) but you need a skipper (the lawyer) to sail you to treasure island. You do not know how long the journey will take and how much it will cost. The skipper tells you his day rate for his ship and his crew and you nearly faint. So you say to him,

"Is there another way? It is a lot of treasure but I cannot afford your day rate right now as I am not made of money." And he says,

"Well, listen, I will do it for free, but once we do find the treasure I will charge you double my hourly rate, yes?"

Well, you see the sense in this but you might be worried just how big this figure is ultimately going to be. Let's say the island is thousands of miles away in the middle of the Pacific and it may take many months to get there. His day rate could be very large, even before it is doubled.

You say to him, "Okay, I see the sense in that, but what if your fees eat up all the treasure and there's nothing left for me? The whole exercise will be a bit pointless."

He says to you, "Good point. Okay, look. I will limit my fees to no more than 25% of your treasure. I will 'cap' my fees. But you are going to have to pick up costs along the way, expenses like port fees, navigator's costs and soldier's pay to protect us from any natives or cannibals on the island or pirates en route.[68] I am not going to pay for these. I have enough to pay for with my ship and my crew."

---

68 Court, expert, barrister's and insurance fees.

You can just about afford these expenses so you agree.

He might say to you, "25% is not enough as the treasure is not big and the journey long and risky. So I want a 50% cap."

Well, you might moan about this, but at the end of the day it is a business partnership, a deal, in which you are getting at least something, instead of nothing, all thanks to his help. You might say to him, "35%, but only if you help me pay these expenses if cash is tight."

And he says, "Okay, deal."

You can see how the amount of treasure (claim value) and the riskiness of the journey (the merits of the claim) are important factors in deciding what percentage to charge.

Now I have mentioned "expenses" above. You should be aware that there is no such thing as a free lunch. You are going to have to put your hand in your pocket to pay for court fees, counsel's advice, if needed, expert's fees and so on. You may also have to pay for "After the Event Insurance" - insurance which protects you from having to pay a large legal bill if you lose, where your opponent is instructed by expensive lawyers, for instance. This insurance pays out the premium in a lump-sum right at the end of the case if you lose and takes a part of your treasure if you win. It will have an up-front fee.

We now also have "damages-based agreements" (DBAs). These are American-style agreements, introduced in 2013.

Going back to the treasure island analogy, in this case the skipper says to you, "Okay, I will work entirely for free, <u>win or lose</u>, but I want 25% of the treasure. Period."

"What about your hourly rate?" you ask. "Aren't you going to charge me anything for all your time and expense?"

"Forget about that", he says. "I'll just do it for a share of the treasure." He then thinks for a minute, "In fact" he adds, "I will even pay all the expenses."

So you see that in the 'no win no fee' arrangement you have the lawyer double his hourly rate and use a cap to make sure his fees do not gobble up all the treasure, but in the case of DBAs, it is very simple – he just takes a share.

DBA sounds just like the ticket, right?

Well, yes, it works for you but does it work for the skipper?

Actually, in the case of the DBA he knows that particular island and he knows the size of the treasure and it is huge. So he is happy to take a risk.

Unfortunately most cases are not like this, and this is why very few skippers are going to agree to a DBA. Unless the claim value is very large - seven figures, let's say - the 'no win no fee' agreement is better for him in every way. This is because of the limitations that were brought in at the time they were introduced. Without boring you with the detail, the 2013 Act made some conditions around DBAs, which rather ham-strung the whole point of them! So that in most average cases lawyers do not touch them! The reason is that the old guard are afraid of our legal system turning into an American-style business market and so are very grudging and slow at changing the law. It will probably take further legislation to advance the process to make them fully-fledged contingency arrangements like they have in the US.

Having said all that, there is an area in which a lawyer may well consider DBAs and that is in small claims of high enough value. This is because you do not usually get your legal costs paid on that track so a CFA will not work, but a DBA with high enough value (let's say anything over £5,000) may be worth it, if they are getting at least 25%-50%. (50% is the limit, inclusive of VAT.) I offered to do one recently with a client who had already done a lot of work on his case.

You could view this as a case where the treasure is not big but the sea journey is very short, just a day's sailing across the bay. So the skipper thinks, "Yeah, why not? I've not got much on at the moment and my crew are bored."

As an alternative to both DBAs and CFAs, you could simply ask a lawyer to "cap" the amount of their legal fees. They would work on a traditional taxi meter arrangement but would agree to not go above a certain amount. For example, they would not go above £4,000 costs in any event in a £10,000 claim. Not many will, but there are enough exceptions to make it worth asking, and lawyers really do need to start moving with the times. There's no harm in asking! If I had a client who was super-organised with a straightforward claim I might well do this type of retainer.

You might also consider bringing in a lawyer half-way. A lot of clients actually do a really great job of initially bringing the claim but then get into choppy weather and suddenly realise they need help.

In that case, a lawyer can turn things around for you - if, after the initial hourly rate work he thinks you have a strong case, he may even do a 'no win no fee' at that point. Or you could just use him to strengthen your case and then drop him for the trial. It's like letting a pilot handle a bit of the journey after take off but before landing in a severe storm or fog whilst you do everything else. It does not stop you taking back the controls afterwards. You may only want to use him where it is essential.

In short, it is good as a litigant in person to have an experienced pilot to hand, who can take over the controls of the plane, if you feel it is necessary. As I said earlier, if a litigation law firm is not prepared to entertain CFAs or DBAs then you really do have to question whether they are properly equipped as a law firm to fight for their clients. If they say, "we don't do them", they are actually limiting your tactical options immediately and significantly, without a thought.

As litigators they should be trying to make sure that there are many options, or weapons, available to you as possible in order to get your claim over the wire. Their retainers can be a key weapon. Opponents facing lawyers who are on 'no win no fee' arrangements know that they are facing a tough opponent – they think the case is strong enough to take it on a contingency basis and will be more determined than the usual lawyers because they will not get paid until they win! A great move in some cases and a way of bringing them to the negotiating table.

To conclude, not all cases are suitable for 'no win no fee'. Where there is not a clear pile of treasure at the end of the journey, or something that can easily be converted into money - like a property or an estate in a will - they are less likely to be of use. To find out whether or not they are suitable, a lawyer is going to have to do some work initially. Sadly, there is no such thing as a "free lunch".

Finally, I should say that there are certain people who waste a lot of my time by phoning up and wanting to spend an hour talking about their case and saying, "This is a sure-fire winner. You need to do it on a 'no win no fee'. It's a great case I've got for you here!" That's nonsense. Not even a lawyer with his own dispute can think in a rational and detached way about its true merits.

You cannot assess a winner unless you have spent at least a couple of hours getting to know the case papers and the client. I have learned this the hard way from having wasted a lot of time on people's hopeless cases in the past. I have also learned that when someone tells me I should do a no win no fee because their claim is a sure-fire winner – this is a good indicator that it is a sure-fire dud.

GLOSSARY

After The Event Insurance: Used with no win no fee cases. This special insurance pays out your opponent's legal costs if you lose. It is usually only payable if you win using your winnings.

Allocation: The point, after statements of case, or pleadings, have been filed or served and is the decision of the court as to whether to send the claim down the small claims, fast, or multi-track. Directions Questionnaires are used to allocate. You can appeal an allocation decision and apply to re-allocate.

Alternative Dispute Resolution (ADR): The courts are big on people trying to settle disputes without going to court. This means any and all methods to achieve this, the most common of which is mediation. But, this also includes arbitration and the newly created, early neutral evaluation. It could also include a formal meeting, or even an online call or conference, whose purpose it is to try and reach a settlement.

Appeal: If you do not like the judgment you get at county court level, you can appeal. This appeal is still likely to be heard at a county court level. You have a strict time-frame in which to appeal and if you think it likely you should ask the judge after judgment for permission to appeal. If it is refused there is then a formal process to apply for leave to appeal.

Budgets: Courts are now big on parties estimating their legal costs of running a claim so that those costs can be kept proportionate and not be allowed to escalate unnecessarily. Thus, parties are required to budget what their costs are likely to be. In multi-track claims you have to complete a Precedent H, and even in fast-track claims a budget may be required by a court order. Litigants in person are not required to produce a Precedent H, but it may, at least, be a good idea to produce a short-form budget and also do not forget to challenge the amount of your opponent's Precedent H if they are represented by solicitors.

Civil Procedure Rules (CPR): The bible on how to run a civil claim. There are other rules for family cases. For personal injury, although they fall within the civil procedure rules, there are quite specific sections that apply to them and this can be complex. Do not forget there are also "Practice Directions" which should be read alongside the rules, to help people implement the rules properly.

Costs Schedules: Costs are a big feature of civil litigation and more important than in other areas of law. At any and every hearing you should be prepared to argue for your costs of that particular hearing if you win and at the end of the claim you should produce a schedule of your entire costs of the whole proceedings. Even if you lose, you might get some of your costs, for instance if you have made an offer early on that is better than your opponent's victory.

Conditional Fee Arrangement ("No Win no Fee"): This is basically a retainer with a solicitor where they are only paid if they actually win. In practice, you will have to find some money. For example, for the early stages when a solicitor is just reviewing your case on its merits and has not decided whether he will do no win no fee, or for disbursements like court fees, expert fees, or barristers. Many barristers, often the good ones, will not do no win no fee and so you need to budget for these additional expenses. Although in practice no win no fee means that you have to part with a percentage of your winnings, the wording of the retainer allows the solicitor to charge a "success fee" which can increase his hourly rate up to 100%. You are then liable for this uplifted part of his hourly rate upon winning. What he does though is cap this uplift at 25% of your winnings so they do not all get gobbled up by this uplift. While the other side are liable for nearly all other costs if they lose (except after the event insurance) they are not liable for the success fee uplift.

Contingency Agreement: Any arrangement with your solicitor where their fees are only paid contingent upon a successful outcome.

Damages-Based Agreement: Another form of contingency arrangement like no win no fee, but more purely taking a percentage of your winnings and nothing else. Only common in very high value cases and sometimes for small claims at the higher end. Because they are a new invention and not really working properly at the current time, you will be lucky to find a solicitor who will do one.

Default Judgment: This usually applies where your opponent ignores your claim. You are unlikely to get it if all they have done is miss a court deadline by a few days. Note that it can often be set aside, sometimes quite easily. If your opponent does this, make sure to hit them with the costs of wasting your time and court time. For instance, you may have to apply to the court using an N244 form for default judgment, which incurs a court fee.

Directions Questionnaire: This is a very important document because it basically lays out the rules of engagement, for instance what track your claim will be on, how long the trial is likely to last, how many witnesses you need and whether you need an expert. You are settling up the parameters of the dogfight so take care with this form and always try and be professional and liaise with the other side.

Disclosure: Civil litigation is split into phases, and the disclosure phase is the key point at which you have to disclose your evidence to the other side. It only happens after the statements have all been filed and served and a court usually will send out an order laying out the disclosure process, although it is also explained in the CPR. The purpose of disclosure is to collect the evidence that you will then use to exhibit as documents to your witness statement, the next phase after disclosure. You can also make an application for disclosure very early, before proceedings are issued, but only do this if there really is critical evidence without which it is impossible to get your claim off the ground. (And you can actually point to this evidence. The courts do not like "fishing expeditions".)

Detailed Assessment: Costs Proceedings, made by means of the Part 8 procedure.

Early Neutral Evaluation: A new type of alternative dispute resolution, that involves an opinion on the strengths of the case, so that parties can more easily come to settlement. It is like a mini or provisional judgment based on what evidence there is at the time. Mediators usually refrain from expressing a view on the merits of a case, which is why it could be a useful alternative to mediation and may grow in popularity in the future as courts come increasingly under strain.

Enforcement: The procedure you follow after you have judgment and want to get your money!

Exhibits: The documents that are the critical evidence that you "exhibit" with your witness statement.

Fast-Track: Claims between £10,000 - £25,000 are usually allocated to the fast track, but be aware it is not automatic and some complex claims or claims with lots of witnesses may be allocated to the multi-track (or conversely allocated down to small claims). For trials of one day.

Fee Remission: You may not have to pay court fees if you are on benefits.

File: Send to court.

Legal Surgery: Something law firms are increasingly pioneering as a low-cost way to get access to a lawyer who will read documents during that hour and is far more feasible by the change to the online world. A necessity these days as legal aid dries up and more and more people have to pay for legal advice.

Letter of Claim: The critical letter that clearly lays out your claim and is an essential precursor to issuing proceedings.

Limitations: Causes of action have time-frames after which you can no longer bring a claim. So typically for personal injury it is 3 years and negligence or contract is 6 years. If you bring a claim out of time it is not necessarily fatal, but a defendant will certainly make a major issue of it in their defence. But the time-frames are not set in stone or absolute.

Litigant in person: Someone who represents themselves in their own case.

McKenzie Friend: Someone who helps a litigant in person run their case, but only in exceptional circumstances will the court allow them to actually do all the work, such as presenting the case in court. They are meant to assist, not take charge.

Mediation: A popular type of alternative dispute resolution that courts are hot on these days. On the small claims track you will be offered mediation and you should probably accept it. In other areas you can do it before proceedings, or you can ask for a stay and do it after pro-ceedings have been issued. It usually takes a day, in the average-sized claim, and can be expensive as you need to pay for a mediator, three rooms, and perhaps your own lawyer if you are using one. In the future of course people may do them online, which will obviously save costs.

Multi-Track: County court claims of a value over £25,000. But remember this is not the only criteria. The trial will be two days or more.

No Win No Fee: See conditional fee agreement. Same thing.

Part 7: Most money claims are made using the Part 7 procedure and are usually basic money claims. Part 8 is for special cases.

Part 36 Offers: Special types of offers which have specific rules if a party fails to beat that offer at trial, leading to the person who has failed to beat an offer (win or lose) taking a big hit on costs. I do not encourage litigants in person to try to master them, but perhaps take some tailored legal advice. This is because they can also use a normal without prejudice offer and a court will also give you benefit for this, though not as much as for Part 36. Do not use them in small claims.

Part 18 Request: A formal way of getting your opponent to ask specific questions, key to your case. This forms part of the pleadings or statements of case and so the judge will be careful to focus on it, more than he would on a simple letter, for instance.

Pleadings: See statements of case.

Practice Directions: To be found alongside the CPR, guidance to help you with the rules and how to follow them properly.

Pre-Action Disclosure: See disclosure, above.

Pre-Action Protocols: The codes enshrined in the CPR which tell you what you have to do pre-issue and the hoops you have to jump through. So do not just shoot from the hip and issue proceedings without having followed the protocols. For most claims the General Pre-action Protocol will apply. (Personal injury claims, larger building disputes and other claims like defamation, for instance, have their own specific protocols.)

Precedent H: See budgets, above. The complex spreadsheet that has to be used in multi-track claims where parties are represented.

Reply: A document that forms part of the statements of case, or pleadings, and is used by a claimant to respond to a defence, or a defendant to respond to a defence to a counterclaim. Not essential, but sometimes helpful in clarifying things you may have missed in your defence or particulars of claim.

Retainers: The fancy word for the contract between you and your solicitor.

Serve: Send to your opponent.

Settlement Agreement: Nearly all cases never go to trial and instead a settlement agreement is drafted, often with a Tomlin order, to bring proceedings to an end.

Small Claims Track: Claims of a value lower than £10,000 and a half-day in length but remember this is not the only criteria, just the main starting point. Trials of half a day. The track where special rules means lawyers are usually (although not always) kept out, because only in exceptional circumstances will you get your legal costs back from the other side if you win.

Statements of Case: Same thing as pleadings. Lays out the factual basis of your case and the basic story and focuses on the relevant issues and is designed to tease these relevant issues out. It is not to be used to give evidence, which is the domain of witness statements. The shorter and more concise the better and the CPR actually requires they be concise.

Strike-Out Application: A powerful weapon that is often used by bigger, well-funded opponents like banks, public bodies and corporations, who will use it to expose weaknesses in your drafted case, even though your case may be at heart a strong one. Bring a claim poorly on the papers and you could face a whopping bill before the plane is even off the ground, as they are often made early on, sometimes even before your opponent has filed a defence. If you lose the hearing you end up having to pay your opponent's costs of that hearing. This acts as a powerful dis-incentive to the faint-hearted to continue with a poorly-drafted claim.

Substantive law: The underlying main law, rather than procedural law.

Summary Judgment: If you think your opponent's case is so weak as to not reach a basic threshold then you can make this early on, often tactically. But be careful, as a judge may be very reluctant to make an early decision without having seen the full evidence, unless of course the opponent looks to be just trying it on, buying time, or is a vexatious litigant.

Trial Bundles: As it says, the bundled set of documents that usually the claimant must produce in advance of the trial and send around to everyone. The court will usually order the timing of this. Allow yourself time as it is more time-consuming than you think and always ensure you liaise with your opponent about what goes in so you do not turn up at court with a bundle your opponent does not agree with. One of those points in the litigation cycle where you need to be professional and co-operate with your opponent.

The White Book: Only barristers should use this hefty legal tome with case authorities on how to interpret the CPR. You can easily go down the rabbit hole with the White Book if you are not a barrister and so better to just focus on the CPR and the plain and common-sense reasoning of the rules and practice directions.

Tomlin Order: The document that is usually required in conjunction with a settlement agreement to formally bring proceedings to an end.

Without Prejudice: What you write on an offer letter which then will not be disclosed until after the judge has made his decision and is considering what costs award he should make. A Part 36 offer is a without prejudice offer.

Without Prejudice Save as To Costs: An offer that is designed to be able to be disclosed in costs proceedings (but not before), should they be necessary on the fast or multi-track.

Witness Statement: Exchanged at a specific date and simultaneously. The document which exhibits your evidence, as opposed to your pleadings or statement of case (which lays out the facts as you say they happened and focuses on the issues). The witness statement is to provide the evidence to prove what you say in your statement of case is right. Do not confuse the two.

ABOUT THE AUTHOR

Alex Woods is a solicitor and litigation specialist with over 25 years of experience in the courts of England and Wales. Since he runs a law firm, he deals daily with all sorts of general litigation, whether representing clients in the courts himself or giving people advice and assistance over the phone when they run their case themselves, just as you may be about to.

Cases that he has worked on include building disputes (acting for both business and individuals), negligence disputes between neighbours, professional negligence (accountants and solicitors), financial mis-selling litigation (suing banks), contractual disputes, landlord and tenant, personal injury, small-scale commercial disputes, cohabitation property disputes, contested will disputes and inheritance act claims. One new area in which Redwood Legal now provides access to justice is representing foreign businesses against UK-based opponents who are trying to use cross-border issues to evade debts.

He passionately believes in access to justice, ever since he came up against the problem of large, rich businesses and corporations who intimidate opponents with the cost of legal proceedings. He first came across this as a young lawyer whilst working for his father's small business in Colchester, Essex, involving a dispute with a well-known construction company. This is why the law firm now specialises in "no win no fee" cases, provides discounted and fixed-fee services for litigants in person, and why it runs a YouTube channel providing people with advice and assistance on running their claims. More recently, it created the CourtWingman (dot) com website.

Sometimes clients do not need full representation and just rely on the free materials or and the odd phone call. Alex Woods likes nothing more than when people are able to run their claims with minimal help. One recent example is a follower who had been faithfully following the free materials on YouTube and had written a long thank-you note, attaching the actual copy of the judgment that had been made in his favour! He had won without paying a penny to lawyers.

Before establishing the law firm, Alex Woods was passionate about financial mis-selling and represented many clients against the banks at the time of the 2008 recession (payment protection insurance and interest rate swaps). He appeared on BBC's popular daytime television show with Angela Rippon, Julia Somerville and Gloria Hunniford, "Rip Off Britain!".

Printed in Great Britain
by Amazon

44334668R00041